THIS BOOK

FOOTBALL 4 EVERY 1

D1341344

70003023136 5

FOOTBALL 4 EVERY 1

Illustrated by Martin Chatterton

PAUL COOKSON

MACMILLAN
CHILDREN'S BOOKS

For Peter Hanratty – The headteacher who turned his school blue. Football, poetry and education sealed the friendship . . . but mostly football!
Paul

To Annie, The Girl From Neston Street who turned out to be a Red.
Martin

Published 2020 by Macmillan Children's Books
an imprint of Pan Macmillan
The Smithson, 6 Briset Street, London EC1M 5NR
Associated companies throughout the world
www.panmacmillan.com

ISBN 978-1-5290-2271-1

Text copyright © Paul Cookson 2020
Illustrations copyright © Martin Chatterton 2020

1 3 5 7 9 8 6 4 2

A CIP catalogue record for this book is available from the British Library.

Designed by The Dimpse
Printed and bound by CPI Group (UK) Ltd, Croydon CR0 4YY

CONTENTS

FIRST HALF

FOOTBALL 4 – EVERY 1	3
THE FOOTBALLER'S PRAYER	4
POEM FOR THE FIRST DAY OF THE FOOTBALL SEASON	6
THE CHOOSING	7
AT HOME	8
FAMILY FOOTY LOOK A LIKES	10
EVERY GAME'S A HOME GAME WITH MY FOOTY FAMILY	11
MY SISTER IS A SUPERSTAR	12
WHEN THE WASP FLEW UP MY BROTHER'S SHORTS	14
DAD'S HAT TRICK CELEBRATIONS	16
DON'T PUT MUM IN GOALS	17
DAD SAID	18
WHEN MY GRANDDAD REFEREES	19
MY GREAT GRAN – THE FOOTBALL FAN	20
SLIDE TACKLE	21
HE JUST CAN'T KICK IT WITH HIS FOOT	22
TIGHT KNIT TEAM	24
GRANNY COULD SCORE THAT	26
LIVE ON THE TELLY	28
OOH AH – MRS CARR	30
DETHRONED	31
PITCH INVASION	32
THE GREATEST GOAL EVER SCORED	33
THE CAT ON THE PITCH	35
A DOG CALLED PICKLES	36

MR KENNING – THE REFEREE   37

DAD DON'T SHOUT AT THE REF   38

UNOFFICIAL WHISTLE   40

NUMBER THIRTEEN   41

THE ODD SQUAD   42

ONE OF THE CROWD   44

NOT THE SOUND OF THE CROWD HE WANTED   45

TEAM OF HEARTS   46

I BELIEVE IN MIRACLES   47

THE FINAL PIECE IN THE JIGSAW   48

NEVER JUST ABOUT THE GOALS   49

THE TACKLE THAT SHOOK THE GROUND   50

THE KING OF THE BOBBLE   51

BAMBOOZLER   52

CULTURED LEFT FOOT   53

RONNIE HAIKU   53

MY FRIEND TOM   53

DEFIANCE   54

SONNET TO THE TEAM I LOVE   55

PETRARCHAN SONNET FOR THE TEAM I LIKE THE LEAST   56

HALF-TIME

PIE QUEUE HAIKU   58

SECOND HALF

THE GOALIE WITH EXPANDING HANDS   60

A.C. ROSTIC – GOALKEEPER   61

NO ONE PASSES ME   62

I DON'T WANT TO BE IN THE WALL   63

COOL-SCORIN' MATCH-WINNIN' CELEBRATIN' STRIKER   64

POETRY IN MOTION   65

WEREWOLF DAD 67

HAIKUS 68

GOAL OF THE SEASON 69

SIXPENCE 70

DRIBBLE 71

CURVE BALL 72

FREE KICK 73

V.A.R. 74

WHOOPS 75

FOOTBALL HAS IT ALL 76

IT'S A GAME OF NUMBERS 77

EATING, SLEEPING, BREATHING . . . ALWAYS LIVING FOOTBALL 78

CURSE OF THE KEEPER 80

NINETEEN SIXTY-SIX 81

THE GRACE THAT LAUNCHED A THOUSAND HIPS 83

ONE MATCH AT A TIME 84

ELEVENS 86

WE BELIEVE IN FOOTBALL 90

BAD BUDGIE 92

CARD HIM, REF! 93

TAKING ONE FOR THE TEAM 94

SUB 94

SATURDAY MEN 95

MAGIC AND LOSS 96

WHO IS THAT MAN? 97

THE MAN IN THE HIGH VIZ VEST 98

THE ROMANCE OF THE F.A. CUP
    (AND WE'RE IN LOVE WITH IT AGAIN) 99

FORTUNE FAVOURS THE BRAVE 101

THE FOOTBALL RESULTS ARE AS FOLLOWS 102

ALWAYS HOPE 103

LEAGUE TABLES 104

ON REFLECTION 105

SHIRT SWAP 106

DON'T GO IN THE CHANGING ROOMS 108

MATHEMATICALLY IMPOSSIBLE, GRAMMATICALLY
   IMPLAUSIBLE 110

WAITING FOR THE FINAL WHISTLE AT ONE NIL UP 111

PERFECT 112

POEM FOR THE LAST DAY OF THE SEASON 113

POST-MATCH RITUALS 114

EXTRA TIME

BLESSED IS THE PEOPLE'S CLUB 116

ABOUT THE AUTHOR AND ILLUSTRATOR 120

FIRST
HALF

FOOTBALL 4 – EVERY 1

So, put the *all* in football
We're all having fun
We all know the score
Football 4 – Every 1

Football 4 – Every 1
Down with h8 – Racism 2
Football is for everyone
Him and her and me and you

Back garden or school playground
Down the local park
Five-a-side under the lights
It doesn't matter where you start

A kick-about with mates
Penalties with Dad and Mum
Keepy-uppies by yourself
Football 4 – Every 1

Everyone can play
Everyone can kick a ball
Jumpers for your goalposts
That's why football has it all

So, put the *all* in football
We're all having fun
We all know the score
Football 4 – Every 1

Football for
Every one
Too

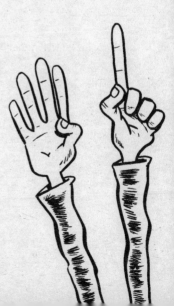

THE FOOTBALLER'S PRAYER

Our team
Which art eleven
Hallowed be thy game
Our match be won
Their score be none
On turf as we score at least seven
Give us today no daily red ... card
And forgive us our lost passes
As we forgive those
Who lose passes against us
Lead us not into retaliation
And deliver us from penalties
For three is the kick off
The power and the scorer
For ever and ever
Full time

4

POEM FOR THE FIRST DAY OF THE FOOTBALL SEASON

Brand-new start
Last season is history and meaningless

My team has no points
And neither has yours

All things are possible
And all glory dreamable

Everything is winnable
Potential is unmissable

The peak of faith is scaleable
The mountain of hope is touchable
The summit of belief, believable

Ten to three on that first Saturday
And nothing dulls the taste

Excitement and anticipation
Tangible and tasteable

Unparalleled success attainable
This could be the best season of our lives

THE CHOOSING

It's in the lap of the gods
Exactly who you are drawn to
The magical moment that decides
Whether you're red, white or blue
You don't choose the football team ...
The football team chooses you

The highs, the lows, the thick and the thin,
Allegiance will always shine through
United you stand together forever
The heart forever is true
You don't choose the football team ...
The football team chooses you

You are special, you are selected,
One of the chosen few
A bond that cannot be broken
There's nothing at all you can do
You don't choose the football team ...
The football team chooses you

AT HOME

It's who we are, it's what we do
It's why we're here, it's me and you
It's where we laugh, it's where we cry
And where we shout and gasp and groan
It's where we meet, week by week
Everton – at home, Everton – at home

At home with those who care
At home with those who dare to dream
More than just a football crowd
More than just a football team

It's church and it's belonging
Weekly mass – communion
It's faith and hope and love and more
It's family, friends, our union

At home we know our places
The special points where we all meet
And all the usual faces
The click clack of a myriad seats

That music before kick off
That heralds expectation
The Z Cars Theme, A Grand Old Team
Excitement, anticipation

Not just what happens on the pitch
Those in blue on Goodison Green
Important landmarks of our lives
Marked by matches we've all seen

Guardians of tradition
We pass that baton on
The heroes of the past
The heroes yet to come

Those magic moments that we shared
The joy and pain we've known
It's where we meet – week by week
Everton – at home

The guiding lights on winter's nights
The Grand Old Lady's throne
It's where we meet – week by week
Everton – at home

Born not manufactured
Never on your own
It's where we meet – week by week
Everton – at home

It's who we are, it's what we do
It's why we're here, it's me and you
It's where we pray – each Saturday
For future hopes unknown
Our history and legacy
Those times to come for you and me
It's where we meet, week by week
Everton – at home, Everton – at home

FAMILY FOOTY LOOK-A-LIKES

Grandad thinks he's Bobby Charlton
    Just because he's bald
Uncle thinks he's Peter Crouch
    Because he's really tall

Just because he wears a cap
    Dad thinks he's Petr Čech
Brother thinks he's Rooney
    Because he looks like Shrek

EVERY GAME'S A HOME GAME
WITH MY FOOTY FAMILY

Grandad's in the goal
Dad's in defence
Mother's in midfield
Baby's on the bench

Sister's centre forward
Brother's at the back
Cousin is the coach
Auntie's in attack

Nana is the manager
And just because I missed
A penalty last home match
... I'm on the transfer list!

MY SISTER IS A SUPERSTAR

She's the girl with the goals –
The Queen of the Green
The undisputed star in our team
Pitch perfect on the pitch
She rules from box to box
We all dance to her tune
As she rolls and as she rocks
Flowing locks, wild and free –
Like a hairy motor biker
My sister is a superstar – a supersonic striker

The Midas touch, the Belle with the ball
The one who wins the hearts of us all
She puts the goal in golden
A jewel in our crown
She dazzles and she sparkles
Running rings around and round
Though they try as they might –
Defenders can't out-psyche her
My sister is a superstar – a super-scoring striker

Top of the shots – the world at her feet
The first name written down on the sheet
The reason for our season
The one who has it all
Every twist and every trick
With her foot and with the ball
Everybody loves her – there's nobody quite like her

My sister is a superstar – a super-scoring striker
My sister is a superstar – a supersonic striker
My sister is a superstar – a scintillating,
 supersonic, super-scoring . . . STRIKER!

WHEN THE WASP FLEW UP MY BROTHER'S SHORTS

A family fun-filled holiday
Seaside football – match of the day
On the beach – the score nine–nine –
When the match went into injury time
We soon forgot our day for sports
When the wasp flew up my brother's shorts

We misread the situation
Thought it was his celebration
Scoring a goal – dancing about
The yell, the scream, the twist and shout
We're all smiles as he cavorts
When the wasp flew up my brother's shorts

The moves he made – we'll never forget
The bottom wiggle and pirouette
The somersaults and acrobatics
A million amateur dramatics
Out of control and out of sorts
When the wasp flew up my brother's shorts

When the wasp flew up my brother's shorts
His eyes bulge wide and his face distorts
Worried where that wasp is caught
Scared of the sting, his body contorts ... but ...
The wasp was the one that was most distraught

Up one leg then down the other
Relief for the wasp, relief for my brother
Took them both a while to recover
Panic attacks and flash back thoughts
When the wasp flew up my brother's shorts

DAD'S HAT TRICK CELEBRATIONS

When Dad scored a goal in the garden
He celebrated with glee
He put his T-shirt over his head
And ran into the tree!

When he scored his second
He should have had more sense
He tried to slide but couldn't stop
And smashed the garden fence!

His hat trick handstand antics tried
To claim the ball and grab it
He slipped and tripped, his trousers ripped
And he flattened next door's rabbit!

When Mum came out and shouted
It was me he blamed
But luckily I'd filmed it
Now it's been on *You've Been Framed!*

DON'T PUT MUM IN GOALS

She'll paint her nails and brush her hair
Can't decide just what to wear
Leave her handbags everywhere
Don't put Mum in goals

Stiletto heels aren't right at all
They might snap and then she'd fall
Even worse – they could burst the ball
Don't put Mum in goals

She might do all these and more
But there's one fact we can't ignore
She never, ever lets us score
Don't put Mum in goals

She dives and stretches, saves and stops
Keeps a clean sheet, calls the shots
Number one – she's the tops
That's why Mum's in goals

DAD SAID

Dad said
He could beat us – blindfolded
With one leg tied behind his back

He was wrong

We ran rings around him
And beat him ten – nine

After extra time

WHEN MY GRANDAD REFEREES

When my grandad referees
He wears his shorts below the knees
Likes the way things used to be
When grandad is the referee

He tells us all of way back when
The good old days when men were men
Shoulder barging was allowed
No one dived or rolled around

He makes us play the old, old way
Three o'clock on Saturday
Rain or shine or snowy weather
With that ball of heavy leather

The imprint of those case-ball laces
Left tattooed on heads and faces
Try to kick it when it's wet
A broken foot is what we'd get

Long hair! He sends us off
Gloves to wear! He sends us off
A little spitting, a little chewing
He sends us off whatever we're doing!

Even worse, it makes us madder
When he uses an old pig's bladder
We don't like what it used to be
When grandad is the referee

MY GREAT GRAN – THE FOOTBALL FAN

My great gran – the football fan
Watches me whenever she can
Never quiet – it's a riot
Always loud with my great gran

She knows the tactics, knows the plan
Shakes her head and waves her hand
Shouts advice that isn't nice
Take his legs! Mark your man!

Cross The Hulk with Desperate Dan
Frankenstein and Jackie Chan
No one's madder, no one's badder
Like an angry Superman

There's no one that's louder than
My great gran the football fan
Disagrees with referees
And now she has a touchline ban

SLIDE TACKLE

It would have been the perfect slide tackle
Had he stopped after getting the ball
But he didn't

He slid off the pitch
Past the manager
And down the tunnel back to the changing rooms

HE JUST CAN'T KICK IT
WITH HIS FOOT

John from our team
Is a goal-scoring machine
Phenomenally mesmerising but . . .
The sport is called football
But his boots don't play at all
Cos he just can't kick it with his foot

He can skim it from his shin
He can spin it on his chin
He can nod it in the net with his nut
He can blow it with his lips
Or skip it off his hips
But he just can't kick it with his foot

With simplicity and ease
He can use his knobbly knees
To blast it past the keeper, both eyes shut
He can whip it up and flick it
Up with his tongue and lick it
But he just can't kick it with his foot

Overshadowing the best
With the power from his chest
Like a rocket from a socket he can put
The ball into the sack
With a scorcher from his back
But he just can't kick it with his foot

Baffling belief
With the ball between his teeth
He can dribble his way out of any rut
Hypnotise it with his eyes
Keep it up on both his thighs
But he just can't kick it with his foot.

From his shoulder to his nose
He can juggle it and pose
With precision and incision he can cut
Defences straight in half
With a volley from his calf
But he just can't kick it with his foot.

He can keep it off the deck
Bounce the ball upon his neck
With his ball control you should see him strut
He can flap it with both ears
To loud applause and cheers
But he just can't kick it with his foot.

He can trap it with his tum
Direct it with his bum
Deflect it just by wobbling his gut
When he's feeling silly
He can even use his . . . ankle
But he just can't kick it with his foot.

TIGHT KNIT TEAM

The football scarf that Grandma knitted
Was so loooooooooooooooooooooooong
That it went round the necks of all our family
Twice
The family next door
Everyone in our street who goes to the match
Plus the first team
The manager
And his assistant

GRANNY COULD SCORE THAT

It was easier to score
Couldn't hit a barn door
What on earth's he aiming for
What's he playing at?
How do you miss an open goal?
He had time to take a stroll
Do you call that ball control?
My granny could score that . . .
And so could next door's cat!

One on one at last he's through
Missed it by a mile or two
Just what is he trying to do?
They've got a welcome mat
How much are we paying him?
Anyone could knock it in
Does he really want to win?
My granny could score that . . .
And so could next door's cat!

Dragged his shot so far wide
Gone right to the other side
Hit the corner flag then died
Where all their fans are sat
Think about it – use your head
Now he's blasted it instead
Skied it high into row zed
My granny could score that . . .
And so could next door's cat!

Never mind your fancy flicks
Don't try any of your tricks
All you have to do is kick
Miss it and I'll eat my hat
A chance so easy I could do it
Both eyes closed – nothing to it
But it was you – and you blew it
My granny could score that . . .
And so could next door's cat!

There it is son – on a plate
Do you need a Sat Nav mate?
How long are you going to wait?
There's no time to chat
You couldn't hit a cow's backside
With a banjo if you tried
Overpaid, undignified
My granny could score that . . .
And so could next door's cat!

LIVE ON THE TELLY

Dad's got his usual seat
I've got the sofa

Replica shirts
Discussing tactics

Bottle of pop
Bags of crisps

Chocolate bars
Chocolate biscuits

Kicking every ball
Tackling every tackle

Half-time rush
For the kettle and toilet

Fists waving
Heads in hands

Complete joy
Utter disbelief

So far away
So closely involved

Not long left
The tension builds

One goal up
The final whistle
YEEEEEEEEEEEEEEEESSSSSSSSSSSSSSSS!!!!!!!!!!!

OOH AH – MRS CARR!

Ooh ah – Mrs Carr!
She's a footy superstar!
Ooh ah – Mrs Carr!
She's a footy superstar

Mrs Carr is great
Mrs Carr is ace
Mrs Carr has always got
A smile upon her face

Always has a ball
Whenever she's in class
Teaching us to shoot
Teaching us to pass

Teaching us her skills
Back heel kicks and flicks
Keepy-uppies, round the world
All her fancy tricks

Nutty about footy
For every boy and girl
She's the greatest teacher
In – the – world!

Ooh ah – Mrs Carr!
She's a footy superstar!
Ooh ah – Mrs Carr!
She's a footy superstar

DETHRONED

Solomon was number one
Soccer's super special son
No one could compete
With his nimble magic feet

The freestyle football master
Nobody was faster
The coolest kid at everything
The keepy-uppy football king

But Odetta – when he met her
Was trickier and better
Fleet of foot and slick and new
So number one was number two

Now de-throned, he lost his crown
To the quickest, slickest girl around
With neverending bouncing ball –
A walking trampoline
The undisputed, football booted
Keepy-uppy footy queen

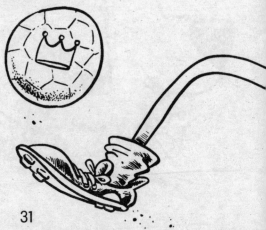

PITCH INVASION

No one had an indication
Of the impending pitch invasion

Ozzy's dog ran on the pitch
Baby brother followed it

Brother wobbled, tumbled down
Worried mummy chasing round

Screaming, shouting as she ran
Zimmer frame – on came Nan

All of them – running free
Then falling on the referee

Very strange, very random
Flattened ref, match abandoned

THE GREATEST GOAL EVER SCORED

I got the ball in my own half
Keepy-uppies – thigh and calf
Beat round one, two, three then four
All the team and then twice more
Every challenge – I ignored
For the greatest goal ever scored

Twists and turns and back heel flicks
Step over and chips and kicks
Ran the full length of the pitch
Hijinx with my skills and tricks
I heard all the crowd applaud
The greatest goal ever scored

Shoot! Volley! Exocet!
Top corner of the net
The best goal of the century
Spectacular and scored by me
Universally adored
The greatest goal ever scored

er . . . we-ell . . .

It wasn't quite like that at all
I tripped up trying to kick the ball
My shorts fell down as I span round
I landed face down on the ground
Everybody laughed and roared
At . . . the greatest goal I ever scored?

Their defender tried to clear it . . .
My backside was quite near it
THWACK! YOW! BADOING! BLAST!
Like a rocket it shot right past
And left the goalie open-jawed
At . . . the greatest goal I ever scored!

All I got was a comedy award
For the funniest goal – ever scored!

THE CAT ON THE PITCH

The black cat on the pitch
Was the most exciting thing about the match

Still didn't bring us any luck
But took a long time for the stewards to catch

A DOG CALLED PICKLES

A national treasure stolen
A national treasure found

Pickles – national superstar
A truly treasured hound

Super pooch and super sleuth
No ordinary pup

Just in time he sniffed and found
The Jules Rimet World Cup

MR KENNING – THE REFEREE

Match starter
Watch watcher
Time keeper
Play stopper

Decision maker
Foul ignorer
Blind eye-er
Game changer

Headline causer
Finger pointer
Penalty giver
Card waver

Crowd incensor
Hassle taker
Abuse listener
No mate-er

Hot seater
Black wearer
Gun sticker
Whistle blower

DAD DON'T SHOUT AT THE REF!

Always just the same
In every single game
I bet that they can hear him in Kiev
Does he have to be so loud?
Louder than the crowd
Dad – don't shout at the ref!

His cheeks are burning red
Each hair stands off his head
Raving without ever taking breath
Yelling and he's screaming
Both his eyes are steaming
Dad – don't shout at the ref!

There's no chance of him stopping
Both his eyes are popping
Cursing like a foul-mouthed TV chef
Jumping when he rants
Like there's scorpions down his pants
Dad – don't shout at the ref!

Always disagreeing
With everything he's seeing
Every little thing leaves him bereft
Sweating most profusely
His tongue is wagging loosely
Dad – don't shout at the ref!

Do you know the rules?
You silly stupid fool!
Are you blind as well as dumb and deaf?
Holding up his glasses
Every time he passes
Dad – don't shout at the ref!

His theory seems to be
It's a conspiracy
Complaining that it might as well be theft
Screaming and a-howling
That no one sees the fouling
Dad – don't shout at the ref!

Because he's inconsistent
He's berating the assistant that a
Fate awaits them that is worse than death
We know his football passion'll
Make him more irrational
Dad – don't shout at the ref!

Mum's partly to blame
When she says it's just a game
And asks him whether all his sense has left
If he doesn't start to stop it
His heart is going to cop it
Dad don't shout
Don't let your anger out
It's not what it's about
DAD – DON'T SHOUT AT THE REF!

UNOFFICIAL WHISTLE

For a little joke, the referee's wife
Embarrassed her bloke in his working life
Exchanged his silver acme whistle
For something much more unofficial

A loud and noisy duck caller
She thought it suited the modern footballer

It didn't seem quite the same
When later in the game
A crudely timed challenge
Halted the attack
Penalty given ...
Quack! Quack! Quack!

NUMBER THIRTEEN

They gave me a number
The number thirteen
The night that I joined
The Halloween Team

An ogre in goals
A zombie who's green
A bat and a cat
And a mummy that's mean

A dragon defender
Letting off steam
A werewolf and vampire
You don't get between

A ghost and a ghoul
With silvery sheen
And lastly and leastly
The beastly thirteen

The oddest of squads
That's ever been seen
I'm number thirteen
In the Halloween Team

THE ODD SQUAD

Here's the goalie – Teflon Tim
Nothing ever sticks to him

Right full back – Ted McFee
Plays like it's nineteen-oh-three

Self-made man – Frankie Stein
He will scare their number nine

Big Norm snacks on referees
Bites yer legs and chews yer knees

Do not pick Desolate Dan
Plays like the invisible man

Mattio Mattio thinks he's a ninja
Just a shame he's always injured

Nasty-tempered, foul-mouthed Fred
He'll see red and lose is his head

Arthur Merlin – skills concealed
Tricky wizard in midfield

On the wing – soo spectacular
You can count on Davie Dracula

Christiano Zoho's either
A drama queen or diva diver

Seldom scores – Jigsaw Cox
Goes to pieces in the box

Boss with bulging eyes and nose
The more he shouts the more it glows

ONE OF THE CROWD

There were really naughty words
When they all sang that song

My mum told me off
When I sang along

NOT THE SOUND OF THE CROWD HE WANTED

He wants the roars and applause
For all the goals he scores

But gets cat calls and hisses
For the chances that he misses

He dreams of all the cheers
Ringing in his ears

Instead – there's jeers and boos
Every time they lose

TEAM OF HEARTS

We may not have won the league
But we all played our parts
And if you love your football
We are the team that won your hearts

I BELIEVE IN MIRACLES

I believe in miracles
I believe the unbelievable
That football can amaze and
Retrieve the un-retrievable

The magic of momentum
The science of the swing
The panic under pressure
The chaos that it brings

When fortune favours bravery
When planets all align
When everything just goes to plan
And this is our time

THE FINAL PIECE IN THE JIGSAW

Slots in neatly
Fits completely
Exactly what we're looking for

The permanent fixture
Completes our picture
The final piece in our team jigsaw

J Spilsbury 9

NEVER JUST ABOUT THE GOALS

A simple pass in a midfield crowd
A crunching tackle that shakes the ground

A penalty save that lifts the heart
A sixty yarder across the park

A step over, a turn or flick
A nutmeg or a scissor kick

A back heel that creates the space
A winger's winning turn of pace

A thumping header to halt an attack
A striker chasing all the way back

A cheeky chip or speed of thought
An offside trap that has them caught

A shoulder drop, a sideways glance
A bounce or bobble, half a chance

All of these and a thousand more
As well as any goals we score

It's never just about the goals
Never just the goals

THE TACKLE THAT SHOOK THE GROUND

Solid as a – road block
Everything came to a stop
Smack! Bump!
Thwack! Thump!
The crowd all heard that sound
The tackle that shook
The tackle that shook
The tackle that shook the ground

No nonsense and no messing
Brute force – no finesse in
The bone shaking
Ground quaking
Avalanche that's rolling down
The tackle that shook
The tackle that shook
The tackle that shook the ground

Blood and mud and sweat and cheers
Grinding through the mighty gears
The onslaught
Of a juggernaut
He'll never let you down
The tackle that shook
The tackle that shook
The tackle that shook the ground!

THE KING OF THE BOBBLE

He's the king of the bobble
The prince of the bounce
That turns a half chance
Into a chance

Watch for the spin
Watch for the wobble
Or you'll lose out
To the king of the bobble

BAMBOOZLER

Bamboozles me
Bamboozles you
Bamboozles everyone else

Confusing and bamboozling
He even confuses himself

Bamboozles left
Bamboozles right
Bamboozles round and round

Confuses and bamboozles
Everybody in the ground

A master exhibitionist
With skills that are fantastic
A trickster and magician
His legs are like elastic

Bamboozles with those twists and turns
Lots and lots and lots and lots
So much so – that we all know
He'll tie himself in knots

CULTURED LEFT FOOT

A phrase the pundits
Always say about the left
But not the right foot

RONNIE HAIKU

Not the best striker
Only scores a goal ev'ry
Seventeen matches

MY FRIEND TOM

Got the rock star flowing locks
Pity about his half-mast socks

DEFIANCE

In an act of defiance
The striker celebrated his goal
By removing his shirt
To reveal
The exact same shirt underneath
Thus confusing the referee

SONNET TO THE TEAM I LOVE

Shall I compare thee to a Saturday
Three o'clock the start in the afternoon
For then I watch my champions at play
Praying that we taste the victory soon
My heart beats wildly in my youthful breast
As we strive forward, onwards, evermore
Attack with vigour, vim and youthful zest
Perchance to shoot, perchance even to score
I swear allegiance to my belov'd team
Though days be dark and bleak as is the night
Perchance to wish, perchance even to dream
Of glories now within our mortal sight
    So long as men can breathe or eyes can see
    We will support the cause and follow thee.

PETRARCHAN SONNET FOR THE TEAM I LIKE THE LEAST

With vengeance and with passion it is true
That there's a football team I love to hate
Whose skills and style I can't appreciate
Because they play in red shirts, not in blue
It's not just me, for thousands feel it too
Although their players may be good or great
It's natural for them to irritate
With arrogance and pride in all they do

I wish upon them losses and defeats
Though there be no logic to my reason
I pray they're thrashed and humiliated
Discontentment ever be their season
May their smug fans be squirming in their seats
Last not least, may they get relegated.

HALF-
TIME

PIE QUEUE HAIKU

Sometimes the only
Thing to look forward to is
The pie at half-time

SECOND
HALF

THE GOALIE WITH EXPANDING HANDS

Any crosses, any shots
I will simply stop the lot
I am always in demand
The goalie with expanding hands

Volleys, blasters, scissor kicks
I am safe between the sticks
All attacks I will withstand
The goalie with expanding hands

Free kicks or a penalty
No one ever scores past me
Strong and bold and safe I'll stand
The goalie with expanding hands

Let their strikers be immense
I'm the last line of defence
Alert, on duty, all posts manned
The goalie with expanding hands

Palms as long as arms expand
Thumbs and fingers ready fanned
You may as well shoot in the stand
Not a chance! Understand?
Number one in all the land
Superhuman, super-spanned
In control and in command
I'm the man, I'm the man
The one and only goalie . . .
With my expanding hands

A.C. ROSTIC – GOALKEEPER

Gargantuan, colossus, somewhat god-like
Omnipresent guardian of the goals
A giant among mortals, superhuman
Lord of the area he patrols
Keeper of the nets, he keeps them empty
Everything he touches he controls
Even shots of thunder and deflections
Perfect timing, joyous to behold
Ever the invincible protector
Reflexes of lightning, touch of gold

NO ONE PASSES ME

I'm a blaster not a tapper
A ninety-minute scrapper
A chopper and a hacker
No one passes me

I've got the brawn and muscle
For the tackle and the tussle
I will hassle and I'll hustle
No one passes me

Harum-scarum do or dare 'em
I will take the knocks and bare 'em
Show me strikers and I'll scare 'em
No one passes me

I'm a winner not a loser
A rough 'em tough 'em bruiser
A goal scorer's confuser
No one passes me

Summer sun or winter mire
Lion-hearted do or die-er
In my belly burns a fire
No one passes me

I'm a last-ditch tackle fighter
A knee and ankle biter
Nobody marks you tighter
Cos NO ONE passes me.

I DON'T WANT TO BE IN THE WALL

There is nothing that is scarier
A free kick on the edge of the area
Ten yards back isn't far at all
I don't want to be in the wall

I don't want to feel that power
And blast at all those miles per hour
Faster than a cannonball
I don't want to be in the wall

Please don't hit me in the face
Or even worse – that lower place
So I crumble, scream and fall
I don't want to be in the wall

Wish I was – far too tall
Wish I was – far too small
Wish I wasn't scared of the ball
I don't want to be in the waaaaaaaaallllllllllll!

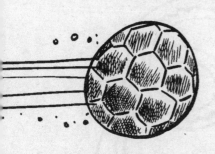

COOL-SCORIN' MATCH-WINNIN' CELEBRATIN' STRIKER

He's a shirt removin' crowd salutin'
handstandin' happy landin'
rockin' rollin' divin' slidin'
posin' poutin' loud shoutin'
pistol packin' smoke blowin'
flag wavin' kiss throwin'
hip swingin' arm wavin'
breakdancin' cool ravin'
shoulder shruggin' team huggin'
hot shootin' rootin' tootin'
somersaultin' fence vaultin'
last minute goal grinnin'
shimmy shootin' shin spinnin'
celebratin' cup winnin' STRIKER!

POETRY IN MOTION

Scorer, striker, artist, entertainer
Special skill standard maintainer
Never boring or mundaner
Highest quality campaigner

Turns on a sixpence
Predatory instincts
Measures any distance
In an instant

Lithe and lean – very acrobatical
A brain for the angles – very mathematical
Regal, royal – aristocratical
Theatrical – very dramatical
Standing ovations – the fans are fanatical

Show me a pair of heels that are cleaner
Or a physique that is leaner
Or a hunger that is keener
Or a finishing touch that's meaner
The grace and poise of a ballerina

Brain of a thinker, balance of a dancer
Ask him a question he's always got an answer
Every opportunity, every half chancer
Can he snap it up – of course he can sir . . .

The jinks, the dinks, the dribbles and the tricks
The deft back heels and the delicate flicks
The punishing power, the bicycle kicks
The perfect placement slickety slick

Through defences, ghostly, haunting
Always dangerous, always daunting
Skill and ability, flair he's flaunting
Easing, teasing, testing and taunting

Pulling all the strings like a classical musician
Knows every trick just like a magician
Makes you feel better like a good physician
Feel the zeal of a man with a mission
Genius in any position
And he's a star you can wish on

He's got a vision, clear and specific
Cold and clinical – very scientific
Takes every chance no matter how diffic –
Ult it is
The same res-
Ult it is

Man of the match – plays like a dream
We just wish he could play for our team.

WEREWOLF DAD

Werewolf dad,
It's not a full moon once a month
But a home match every two weeks.

He gradually changes,
Once inside the ground he fidgets and twitches,
Dribbles on his scarf and pie.

Just before kick off
The veins on his neck stand out
And he bounces up and down on the spot.

It's three o'clock and the change is complete,
The whistle blows and that's it . . .
Howling and barking at the men in the middle.

Mild-mannered dad
To mad werewolf football fan
In ninety minutes plus injury time.

HAIKUS

The crowd is full of
Big men in replica shirts
Wishing they were stars

Shouting loud advice
On how to play the game when
They can't play themselves

GOAL OF THE SEASON

Unstoppable – a belter
A real goal-net melter

Unreachable – a stinger
A sizzling humdinger

Unsaveable – a blaster
A hundred mile right past you

Untouchable – a screamer
A centre forward's dream-er

Unforgettable – a scorcher
A form of goalie torture

Unrepeatable – a winner
A never quite the same again-er

Unique – the reason
The goal of the season

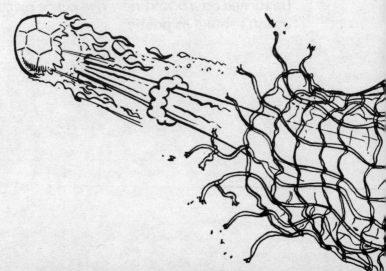

SIXPENCE

They said
He turned on a sixpence

But we don't know
What a sixpence is

Apparently, it's a really old coin
Which is very, very tiny

Thus implying innate skill
Fleet of foot deft deception

Dexterity, gymnastic elasticity
And general all-round trickery

In the player's ability
To turn on the ball in a very compacted area

Still . . .

He turned on a brand-new five pence piece
Doesn't sound as poetic

DRIBBLE

Dribbling around half their team
Twice
He dribbled into the penalty area
Around the keeper
And into the net

If only he'd had the ball
It would have been so much better

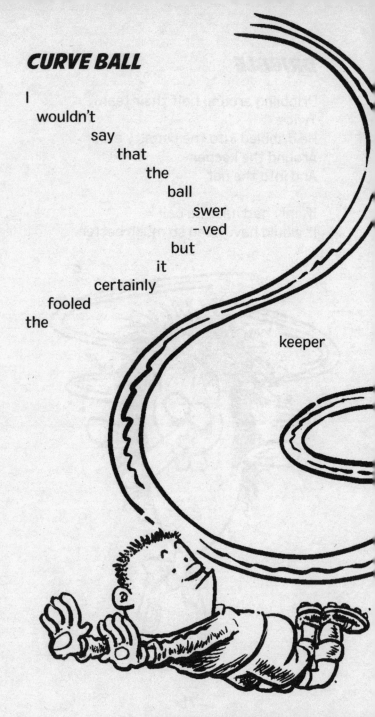

CURVE BALL

I
wouldn't
say
that
the
ball
swer
- ved
but
it
certainly
fooled
the

keeper

FREE KICK

He sliced it
Into the man at the end of the wall
Who deflected it in the opposite direction
Where it hit the keeper's left foot
Bounced onto a post
Then on a defender's backside
Up to the cross bar
Where it dropped
And the spin took it
Eleven millimetres over the line

Now that's what you call a
Freak
Kick

V.A.R.

If you really slow it down
Really, really slow it down
And watch it frame by frame by frame
You can clearly see
The defender's outstretched little finger
Brush the striker's elbow
Thus affecting momentum
Causing him to lose his footing
At the vital moment
Roll over fourteen times
While holding his face

Definite penalty

Very
Awkward
Replay

WHOOPS

A simple shot the keeper dropped

Striker ran in – got a tap in

Easily

FOOTBALL HAS IT ALL

History and legacy
Champions and trophies
Heroes and villains
Football has it all

For the people by the people
Universal language
Truly international
Football has it all

The World Cup in the playground
Wembley in our gardens
Premier League in every park
Football has it all

Memories to cherish
When all time stood still
The bookmarks of our lives
Football has it all

So much we can learn from
So much it can teach us
So very many dreams
Football has it all

IT'S A GAME OF NUMBERS

Four four two
Three five three
Eleven v eleven

Three o'clock
Ninety minutes
Forty-five each way

Three points, one point, zero
Score one more than them
It's a game of numbers

Front two
Flat back four
Big number nine

Fifty thousand cheering
Hundred grand a week
Multi-millionaires

Four two
Number one
Sixty-six
It's a game of numbers

EATING, SLEEPING, BREATHING...
ALWAYS LIVING FOOTBALL

Eating, sleeping, breathing
Always living football
Growing up and basking
In the dreams of sixty-six

Every Christmas, every birthday
Anything with football was acceptable
The Chad Valley Soccer Stadium, shiny
    metal, levers
I never loved Subbuteo

Preferring the steel ball bearing
Travelling with power and speed
Looking more like something
Bobby Charlton may have kicked

The Wembley Trophy football
Casey in waiting
Superior and heavier
The future was orange

Heroes caught mid stride
In countless books and annuals
All mutton-chops and mud
Tight shorts and flowing glam-rock hair

Esso coins and badges
Trying to complete the set
Always one elusive
Took ages to swap our spares and get

And the football pitch that dad built
Creosote markings on our back garden
White posts, real nets that billowed
Like Goal of the Season on Match of the Day

Every Saturday at 'The Rec'
Muddy kneed and laughing
Fourteen a side until it's dark
And first to thirty wins

Eating, sleeping, breathing
Always living football
Always so much more
Than just a game for us to play

CURSE OF THE KEEPER

One mistake – is all it takes
Remembered forever – forgotten – never
And the fingertip saves
The diving of the brave

The goal line blocks
The penalty stops
The superhuman stretch
That no one expects

The unbelievable spectaculars
The reaches most miraculous
Game changing feats
Rendered obsolete

A lapse of concentration – just one
And that's your reputation – all gone
Anywhere else on the pitch
You probably get away with it

Any other position
A different proposition
Miss a sitter or lack of control
Doesn't always lead to a goal

Curse of the keeper
Hero to zero
Who'd be a goalie
Only a hero

NINETEEN SIXTY-SIX

July 30th, Wembley Stadium
Proud in red and white
Alf Ramsey's wingless wonders
Courageous in the fight.
Hurst the hat trick hero
Banks between the sticks
The glory of the story
Nineteen sixty-six

Cohen, strong, unbeatable
Wilson, sharp and in control
Big Jack towers at the back
Moore, the faultless Captain's role
The English Pele – Charlton
The magic match and mix
The grinning of the winning
Nineteen sixty-six

Peters, quiet, studious
Ball runs miles and miles
Hunt the perfect predator
Nobby's toothless smiles
All for one and one for all
Everything just clicks
Forty years of cheers
Nineteen sixty-six

Losing, winning, drawing
A game of highs and lows
The theatre of extra time
The goals, the ebbs and flows
They think that it's all over
Some fans are on the pitch
Glorious, victorious
Nineteen sixty-six

It will never be all over
Everything just fits
History we witnessed
The famous crimson kits
4 – 2 the magic scoreline
Putting on the Ritz
Forever we'll remember
All the twists and kicks
England, Champions of the world
Nineteen sixty-six

THE GRACE THAT LAUNCHED
A THOUSAND HIPS

(For Johann Cruyff)

No man can turn like Johann can
That swivel, twist and back heel flips
Defenders dazzled by the turn
We tried to emulate and learn
The grace that launched a thousand hips

The skill that gave us all a thrill
That no one can outshine, eclipse
Inspired us all to imitate
Your expertise and twist of fate
The grace that launched a thousand hips

The stuff of folklore, legend or
The moment of World Championships
Forever you will always be
Remembered in our history
The grace that launched a thousand hips

ONE MATCH AT A TIME

Same old England, same old fears
Let us down for all these years
1966 – a distant shrine
Overpaid – underachieving
Flattering and still deceiving
Most of us had stopped believing
One match at a time

Weary from the dream that kills us
Hoping that the football thrills us
Disappointment fills your heart and mine
Respect expected – yet un-earnt
Egos crashed, stars that burnt
Mistakes repeated and unlearnt
One match at a time

So – a manager of trust required
A man who some thought uninspired
Marks and Spencer-ly attired design
From the many, chose the few
Out – the old, in with the new
Strength and expectation grew
One match at a time

No egos but equality
A band of brothers – twenty-three
Dignity and destiny align
Sleeping lions far too long
We never dared to sing that song
Slowly though you proved us wrong
One match at a time

Those ghosts and demons from the past
Penalties – we've won at last
Laid to rest – it's got to be a sign
Hopes rise higher with each game
Everybody feels the same
At last we've found and lit that flame
One match at a time

Where no one this time is a scapegoat
And it's more than just that waistcoat
Now there's hope that we at last can shine
So thanks for all the twists and turns
Thanks to you, our love returns
We fan the flames, the fire still burns
One match at a . . .

Time to write our brand-new story
Time to chase our blaze of glory
One more mountain we have yet to climb
Ties that we can never sever
Time to stand and come together
Dream this dream we had forever
One match at a time
We're going to do it
Going to do it
Every time you put us through it
Going to do it
One match at a time

ELEVENS

Poems that mostly use eleven words only and reflect football team formations.

If we all stand on the line perhaps they won't score

somehow

I don't

think

our
formation
is balanced

enough to
work

we

all | get | on | well

in | our | team | except

for

him

formation
play

whatever

we
I
up

seem
always
being

to
end

substitute

our
manager
have a

clue

doesn't
about

what

system
to
play

wearesolidatthebackbutnogoodup

front

last
week   our   manager tried   to
play   our   five   substitutes as well
but   we   still   lost

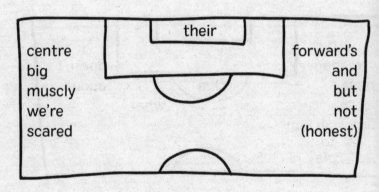

their
centre   forward's
big   and
muscly   but
we're   not
scared   (honest)

every
shot   we   had
was   off   ta
nowhere near
the

goal

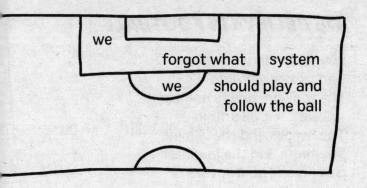

we forgot what system we should play and follow the ball

captain's our mad always get sent OFF! for fighting and ?*X*!!*ing

89

WE BELIEVE IN FOOTBALL

A ninety-minute drama
Each story yet untold
The tension, twists and turns
We watch it all unfold
The heroes and the villains
The tears and the laughter
But no one guarantees
A happy ever after

The past is always with us
Those ties we cannot sever
The triumphs and the tragedies
That bring us all together
The legacy of legends
Both on and off the pitch
We all know our history
Munich, Hillsborough, Sixty-Six

The deftness and the touches
The balance and control
Telepathic vision
The special wonder goal
The something out of nothings
These mesmerising tricks
We practise in the playground
What's perfect on the pitch

Artisans and artists
Creative and instinctive
Old masters and young mavericks
Style and poise distinctive
Admired time and time again
We marvel at the art of it
Each picture tells a story
So glad we are a part of it

We believe in hope
We believe in dreams
Anything is possible
The future yet unseen
On any given match day
Eleven v eleven
We could punch above our weight
Be in football heaven

Be it baggy shirts and brylcreem
A mullet or moustache
Football equals stylishness
Each little touch of class
This game that we call beautiful
The craft, technique and guile
Whatever the result
Let's win or lose in style

BAD BUDGIE

The budgie has learnt naughty words
Where did he get them from?
He got them from my dad
When he had the football on

CARD HIM, REF!

They said he was a card happy ref
And he was

Carded all our team

Four had birthdays
One was getting married
Three were leaving at the end of the season
Two were moving house
And one had a christening

Plus, one was an early Valentine
For the manager
And we are all on his Christmas list

TAKING ONE FOR THE TEAM

Well, of course he did
We'd all take one for the team
That's why we're a team

SUB

Not seen at first
Waiting for my moment
Out of view
Until the time is just right

To make my appearance
Shoot on sight
That's why they call me
Super Sub

Well ...
That and the fact that I'm good at diving

SATURDAY MEN

We are the Saturday men
Three o'clock we come alive

The kick off and the kicks
The rush of blood and thunder

The mud and the leather
The excitement and the unpredictability

The two-act drama over ninety minutes
A play of two halves, no one knows the finale

On the pitch or in the stands
We live for three o'clock

Because we are the Saturday men
The Three o'clock kick off Saturday Men

MAGIC AND LOSS

The magic of the FA Cup
The giant killing dream
Everyone wants an upset but
Not against their team

The romance of the fight
The tie that steals the scene
Everyone wants an upset but
Not against their team

The magic of the FA Cup
The giant killing dream
Everyone wants an upset but
Not against their team

WHO IS THAT MAN?

The man next to the man
Next to the man
Next to the man
Next to the man
Next to the Assistant Man-
Ager next to the Main Man-
Ager?

Just who is he?
And what does he do?

THE MAN IN THE HIGH VIZ VEST

The referee knocked over
The steward in the high viz vest

Sorry he said
Didn't see you there

Then booked him for obstruction

THE ROMANCE OF THE F.A. CUP
(AND WE'RE IN LOVE WITH IT AGAIN)

The year of the underdogs
Where giants have been killed
The Davids beat Goliaths
Fantasies fulfilled
Anything is possible
Two teams of eleven men
The romance of the F.A. Cup
And we're in love with it again

The one-off match, the leveller
The great crash down to earth
Dreams become reality
Wembley's hallowed turf
When minnows swim against the tide
Ride the storm and then
The romance of the F.A. Cup
And we're in love with it again

Those who dare believe may win
And punch above their weight
Blood and sweat and tears and luck
All decide their fate
This year it's for the every man
There's no us and them
The romance of the F.A. Cup
And we're in love with it again

Last gasp shots, deflections
The woodwork and the saves
The referee's decisions
Favouring the brave
Like Ronnie Radford in the mud
The best since way back when
The romance of the F.A. Cup
And we're in love with it again

FORTUNE FAVOURS THE BRAVE

Fortune favours the brave
A smash and grab goal and penalty save
A brilliant stop and the crowd forgave
This week's hero, last week's knave
It may have been a close close shave
Thanks to the woodwork we can crave
All three points and shout and wave
We can chant and we can rave
Fortune favours the brave

THE FOOTBALL RESULTS ARE AS FOLLOWS

The Football Results are as Follows

The game was	1	derful hope you enjoyed it
I don't know if	5	ever seen a better match be
Now I'm feelin'	0	not just because of the pie I
Scoring that many's	7	but hell for them because we
At least we reached our po	10	tial with our talented first
All their supporters are	6	as parrots they just couldn't g
Playing with total	3	dom we will always domin
We were vir	2	uosos, they could not sur

ALWAYS HOPE

Our team plays every week
But we never, ever win
There's always hope and we can't wait
To play next week again

LEAGUE TABLES

We may not be top of the league
As far as points that were achieved
But other aspects of the game
We put our rivals to shame

Goals conceded
A hundred and eleven
Goals scored
Seven

Half-time oranges eaten
None
Chocolate bars and fizzy drinks
Three thousand and thirty-one

Dads sent off for shouting
A whopping twenty-four
Mums who've been much worse
At least eleven more

We may not be top
Okay – we are bottom
Depends on how you look at it
But we won't be forgotten

ON REFLECTION

Free kicks that should have never been
Fouls against us never seen
Penalties not given, easy chances missed
All the goals we were denied
All the times we weren't offside
Everything's against us – we'll add them to the list

Those who should have seen a red
But stayed on to score instead
Incompetence of linesmen and useless referees
The bounces off the post and bar
So very near – and yet so far
It's all tiny margins – blinkered memories

A goalie's gift in stoppage time
Clearances right off the line
The timing of the first goal – things didn't go our way
That decision changed the game
Went against us once again
We could have scored three or four on a different day

Heard the clichés all before – he
Always spouts the same old story
Everyone's against us, this division's tough
But – to quote an old cliché
At the end of the day
It's not that we were robbed . . .
We just weren't good enough

SHIRT SWAP

I just couldn't wait
To swap shirts at full time

My brother's been sick
All over mine

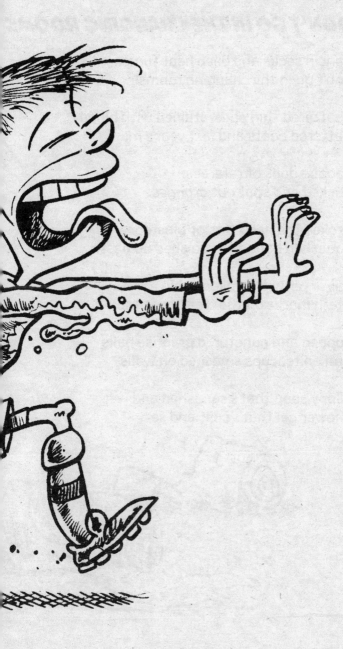

DON'T GO IN THE CHANGING ROOMS

Rancid socks and deep heat fumes
Don't go in the changing rooms!

Shattered shin pads, stained with blood
Battered boots and last year's mud

Voodoo dolls of referees
Sucked and spat out *orangeez*

Broken toe nails, bits of plaster
Squashed bananas, squished up pasta

Hairdryer with broken cable
Teeth marks on the treatment table

Popped and punctured practise balls
Broken teacups smashed on walls

Slippy soap that's squashed and wet
Shower gel that's spilt and set

Sprays and ointments on the shelf
Goalie glove – all by itself

Bandages and toilet rolls
Towels fester, growing mould

The striker's hair band – bright and pink
The full back's underpants – that stink

Smelly socks and deep heat fumes
Don't go in the changing rooms!

MATHEMATICALLY IMPOSSIBLE, GRAMMATICALLY IMPLAUSIBLE

We all know what he really meant
The lads gave a hundred and ten per cent

They tried as hard as they possibly could
The boys done good

WAITING FOR THE FINAL WHISTLE AT ONE NIL UP

I'd bite my nails – but they're all gone
Chewed them down – one by one

The clock has stopped – or even worse
It's going backwards – in reverse

I don't believe in a god anyway
I don't believe but I'm starting to pray

I want to press fast forward –
But everything's so slow
Waiting . . . waiting . . . waiting . . .

For the final whistle to blow

PERFECT

Perfect.
Innocuous at first,
The ball looping over,
No real danger, nothing much on.

But he saw it first,
Acting instinctively and swiftly,
Stretching every single muscle
To claim first touch, the decisive kick.

Couldn't have been placed better . . .
The unreachable arc of the ball
Spinning about the stranded guardian
In slow, slow, s l o o o w w w motion.

The billow of the net from the kiss of the ball,
Perfect.
Well it would have been
If it had been at the other end of the pitch.

POEM FOR THE LAST DAY OF THE SEASON

It looked so good
Halfway through
Unfulfilled
Potential blue

Early exits
From each cup
Safe and sound
But not quite up

We could have done
So much more
Lost too many
Couldn't score

Signs of hope
With good reason
Same time same place
Next football season

POST-MATCH RITUALS

Going through the match afterwards with Dad,
Almost kick by kick.

The what ifs, the nearly goals,
The almost theres and the
How things might have been different.

Savouring the glorious flavours of victory
Or searching for the something sweet
Among the bitter taste of defeat.

Either way the rituals are the same
Going through the match afterwards with Dad,
Almost kick by kick by kick . . .
By kick by kick . . . by kick . . .

EXTRA TIME

BLESSED IS THE PEOPLE'S CLUB

Blessed are the tea makers
Burger fryers, meat pie bakers
Turnstyle turners, ticket takers
All the movers, all the shakers
Blessed are the boot scrapers
The ones who push the mowers
Water sprinklers, grass growers
The ones who keep the pitches clean
The ones who paint the white on green
Those who serve in canteens
All of those who work unseen
All the ladies, all the fellas
Toffee girls and programme sellers
The ones who are the central hub
Blessed is the People's Club

Blessed are the traffic directors
Litter pickers, rubbish collectors
All the stewards who respect us
All the high viz jacket wearers
All the information sharers
Those who lay the tables
Those connecting cables
Those who help the ones who help the ones
Who are less abled
Those who show us to our seats
Those who make our day complete
Those who sell the snacks we eat
Those who cook, then serve the grub
Blessed is the People's Club

Blessed are the ones whose work
Is to brush away the dirt
The ones who wash and press the shirts
Those who brave the post match fumes
Just to mop the changing rooms
The ones who iron corner flags
And unfold all the netting
The ones who paint the goal posts white
And the others we're forgetting
Remember them and so we should
We'd all do it if we could
Blessed is the People's Club

Blessed are the ones who cheer
Year on year on year on year
Those who buy their tickets weekly
The loud, the proud, the mild, the meekly
Those who carry on discretely
Absolutely and completely
Those who travel far and wide
Wear the badge and scarf with pride
Start off early – get back late
The sacrifices that they make
All the time commitment takes
Those with every ticket stub
Those who cheer on down the pub
Blessed is the People's Club

Those who shout out from the stands
Cheer, applaud and clap their hands
Every woman, every man
Every grandad, every gran
Every dad and every mam
Uncle John and Auntie Pam
Nephews, nieces, cousins and
Brothers, sisters – all the clan
All part of our family plan
All the ones who understand
All are welcome – none are snubbed
Blessed is The People's Club

Blessed are the hallowed names
Who walked on water, changed the games
Hanging in the halls of fame
Those memories relived again
Those foundations of our past
Built to lead and built to last
Immortalised in history
Spoken of in reverie
Heroes here for you and me
Those who toiled and gave their all
Fought for every single ball
Those who answered every call
Those who always understood
Blessed is the People's Club

Those who were just passing through
Those who had a job to do
Who only played a game or two
Even they chose royal blue
Those who played and made the grade
Those that shine and those that fade
Bit part extras in the shade
Those who went and those who stayed
Those that got to live our dreams
Trained and managed, picked the teams
All important in the schemes
All the great and all the good
Blessed is the People's Club

Everyone who plays their part
Carries us within their heart
In the light and in the dark
All supporters – true and loyal
Proud to choose the blue that's royal
From the Chairman and the board
To the ones who sweep the floors
All of these – and us – and more
Irrespective of the score
Whether we win, lose or draw
We all know what we're here for
We all know our history
Know the place where we should be
It is you – it is me
It is us – it is we

ABOUT THE AUTHOR

Paul has been writing poems about football all his life. He is Poet In Residence for The National Football Museum and Everton In The Community.

He has been a poet for thirty years and an Everton fan for nearly twice that time.

He still spends most days performing in schools, libraries and festivals and treating the audience like a cheering football crowd.

For more information you can look at his website www.paulcooksonpoet.co.uk or follow him on Twitter @paulcooksonpoet

ABOUT THE ILLUSTRATOR

Martin Chatterton has been successfully writing and illustrating for over thirty years. He has written dozens of books for children and illustrated many more, collaborating with a number of illustrious authors along the way, including several Children's Laureates and global publishing phenomenon, James Patterson. His work has been published in fourteen languages and has won or been shortlisted for numerous awards in Australia, the US and the UK.

His website is www.worldofchatterton.com